AN IDEAS INTO ACTIC

Delegating Effectively

A Leader's Guide to Getting Things Done

IDEAS INTO ACTION GUIDEBOOKS

Aimed at managers and executives who are concerned with their own and others' development, each guidebook in this series gives specific advice on how to complete a developmental task or solve a leadership problem.

LEAD CONTRIBUTOR	Clemson Turregano
CONTRIBUTORS	Gloria Bernabeu, Anand Chandrasekar, Shirley Landry, Kim Leahy, Don Prince, Ron Rabin, Bertrand Sereno
DIRECTOR OF ASSESSMENTS, TOOLS, AND PUBLICATIONS	Sylvester Taylor
MANAGER, PUBLICATION DEVELOPMENT	Peter Scisco
EDITORS	Stephen Rush Karen Lewis
ASSOCIATE EDITOR	Shaun Martin
COPY EDITOR	Tammie McLean
DESIGN AND LAYOUT	Joanne Ferguson
COVER DESIGN	Laura J. Gibson Chris Wilson, 29 & Company
RIGHTS AND PERMISSIONS	Kelly Lombardino

CCL No. 454

ISBN No. 978-1-60491-154-1

CENTER FOR CREATIVE LEADERSHIP

WWW.CCL.ORG

Delegating Effectively

A Leader's Guide to Getting Things Done

Clemson Turregano

Center for
Creative
Leadership®

THE IDEAS INTO ACTION GUIDEBOOK SERIES

This series of guidebooks draws on the practical knowledge that the Center for Creative Leadership (CCL) has generated since its inception in 1970. The purpose of the series is to provide leaders with specific advice on how to complete a developmental task or solve a leadership challenge. In doing that, the series carries out CCL's mission to advance the understanding, practice, and development of leadership for the benefit of society worldwide.

CCL's unique position as a research and education organization supports a community of accomplished scholars and educators in a community of shared knowledge. CCL's knowledge community holds certain principles in common, and its members work together to understand and generate practical responses to the ever-changing circumstances of leadership and organizational challenges.

In its interactions with a richly varied client population, in its research into the effect of leadership on organizational performance and sustainability, and in its deep insight into the workings of organizations, CCL creates new, sound ideas that leaders all over the world put into action every day. We believe you will find the Ideas Into Action Guidebooks an important addition to your leadership toolkit.

Table of Contents

IN BRIEF

In today's organizations, leaders are neither able nor expected to do everything themselves. The consequences of trying to do so can be dire. That's why the ability to delegate effectively—to assign new projects and responsibilities to individuals or a team and providing the authority, resources, directions, and support needed to achieve the expected results—is an essential leadership skill. Delegation starts with creating an environment of trust and dialogue reflecting your understanding of your colleagues and the tasks that need to be accomplished. Delegation is not simply task assignment; rather, it involves giving someone the authority to do something that is normally part of the leader's job. Effective delegation is the mark of a good leader who has developed his or her team members, direct reports, and even supervisors to readily accept and excel at myriad challenges. It is important for work efficiency as well as effectiveness. Effective delegation contributes to teamwork, demonstrating trust, and sharing authority, allowing all team members to participate in a task. This guidebook outlines the benefits of effective delegation and the fears and concerns that can prevent or hinder it, then offers four key ideas that leaders can use to enable better delegation.

Why Delegate?

Have you ever found yourself asking, "Why do I always seem to be doing all the work?" In today's organizations, leaders are neither able nor expected to do everything themselves. The consequences of trying to do so can include burnout, missed deadlines, working long hours, being stretched too thin, and lacking the proper skills needed to complete a particular task. Failing or refusing to delegate can even contribute to a leader's derailment—being fired or demoted or reaching a career plateau. Effective delegation is largely about being able to relate to people in productive ways, and the inability to do so is the most common reason for derailment.

These are all reasons why the ability to delegate effectively—to apportion the work among the people you supervise—is an essential leadership skill and responsibility in fast-changing environments that require high initiative and quick responses from frontline employees.

Delegating involves assigning new projects and responsibilities to individuals or a team and providing the authority, resources, directions, and support needed to achieve the expected results. Delegating is more than merely telling someone what to do. Issuing orders demands compliance; it does not engender commitment or contribute to job satisfaction. People are likely to have more commitment to implementing a decision when they feel they have ownership of the decision and are accountable for its consequences. Delegation starts with creating an environment of trust and dialogue reflecting your understanding of your colleagues and the tasks that need to be accomplished.

Nor is delegation simply task assignment, which is allocating work to an individual that falls within the realm of his or her usual duties and responsibilities. Rather, delegation involves giving someone the authority to do something that is normally part of the leader's job.

The Center for Creative Leadership, in its work with thousands of leaders over a period of more than forty years, has developed some ideas about delegation that will be helpful for you. This guidebook outlines the benefits of effective delegation and the fears and concerns that can prevent or hinder it, then offers four key ideas that leaders can use to enable better delegation.

Getting Started

As a first step, it might be helpful to get an idea of how effective you currently are as a delegator. You can use the Delegating Scorecard to rate yourself.

Many leaders perceive the key benefit of delegating as simply getting something off their desk. But that is just the start. You may get it off your desk, but where does it go from there?

Effective delegation is the mark of a good leader who has developed his or her team members, direct reports, and even supervisors to readily accept and excel at myriad challenges. It is important for work efficiency as well as effectiveness. Effective delegation contributes to teamwork, demonstrating trust, and sharing authority, allowing all team members to participate in a task. This participation is an essential step toward creating interdependence, a key indicator of high-performing teams. Effective delegation can also result in better decisions when competent individuals or teams are closer than the leader to a problem and have more timely information about it. In addition, effective delegation can provide individuals professional growth opportunities; enhance their value to the organization, confidence, self-image, and ultimately self-esteem; and offer more opportunities for people to learn new skills as they struggle with a challenging task that requires them to exercise initiative and problem solving.

Delegating Scorecard

Rate how effective you think your performance has been as a delegator and identify your strengths and challenges. The scale ranges from 1 (not very descriptive of me) to 5 (very descriptive of me).

_____ 1. If others were asked, they would say I am a good delegator.

_____ 2. I delegate tasks to those who will most benefit and develop from the assignment.

_____ 3. I am aware of which kinds of tasks the individuals on my team are best able to accomplish.

_____ 4. When delegating, I involve the individual or team in identifying the desired process and outcomes.

_____ 5. When something goes wrong with a task I delegated, I give the individual or team a chance to work it out first.

_____ 6. When delegating, I brief the individual or team on all the details of the assignment, including its purpose.

_____ 7. When delegating, I make sure all those involved know their own and others' roles.

_____ 8. When delegating, I make sure everyone involved knows the expectations for accountability.

_____ 9. Working with the individual or team assigned the task, I discuss who should be consulted and why.

_____ 10. When the task is completed successfully, I reward the person or team responsible.

_____ Total

If your score is 41 to 50, you're on the right track; keep up the good work. If you scored between 30 and 40, look at where you scored low and develop some insights to help you improve in those areas. If you scored below 30, you definitely need to work on your delegating skills. Regardless of where you scored, reading this book and putting its ideas into practice will help you improve.

Research from many different sources identifies five significant benefits that emerge from effective delegation:

- freeing the leader's time for greater creativity and innovation
- creating trust within the work team
- enabling direct reports to develop as leaders
- providing employees autonomy to accomplish missions, thus increasing the innovation, communication, and creativity of the team
- enabling greater productivity through a shared workload

Effective delegation can result in better decisions when competent individuals or teams are closer than the leader to a problem and have more timely information about it.

Delegation allows leaders to work on more complex and demanding issues. Your identification of others for accomplishment of key tasks demonstrates your trust in them and how they will work to support you and the team. When others accomplish these tasks, even if they stumble along the way, it demonstrates their desire to develop as leaders. This demonstrated capacity for greater responsibility manifests itself in increased motivation and communication, allowing for greater innovation within your team. Instead of your doing all of the tasks yourself, you share the workload with others, demonstrate trust in your team's competence, and most important, develop their trust in your leadership.

Delegating Roadblocks

If all of this seems obvious and clear-cut, then why don't more leaders delegate effectively? There are two major reasons. The first is a strong fear of failure. Delegation involves giving people the discretion to determine how to do a task without undue interference, but it is only natural for a leader to be concerned about the quality of the output or the ability of the person or team to handle problems along the way. We all know leaders who have a hard time letting go and seriously struggle with this aspect of delegation. Maybe they fear the work won't get done, or worse, that it won't meet their standard of perfection. They tend to be in this position because they have proved to be conscientious, they make few mistakes, and they have good ideas. Not surprisingly, they often fear that sharing work responsibilities with others, risking others' mistakes, or being seen as relegating the role of the idea person will be damaging to their career.

To achieve the potential benefits of delegation, leaders need to be competent at finding a good balance between autonomy and control. Monitoring too closely will send a message of a lack of trust in the other person's ability, but abdicating all responsibility may contribute to failure and frustration for the person or team assigned to the task. The leader should explain clearly the amount of discretion to be allowed, which should reflect the skills and experience of the people who are empowered. The leader should also make clear why he or she wants to delegate the task and how it will benefit the assignee.

The second reason that many leaders do not effectively make the transition to accomplishing work through others is because they have never been taught the steps for effective delegation. Many leaders stop short of delegation not because they don't understand the vision, strategy, or goals of the company or because they fail to grasp the need for the task; rather, they do so because

11

they do not understand themselves or their own teams. They don't know when to allow team members to work on projects they can handle. They wonder when to increase the complexity of assignments, not understanding which individuals stand a good chance of succeeding. They tend to keep the same individuals tied to the same team roles and responsibilities. Leaders who are locked into this type of thinking can't explore new perspectives, with the result that they lose the commitment of their teams and find themselves wondering why team performance suffers.

Some leaders who have not learned to delegate may not understand the full cost of their hesitation to do so. Beyond being overworked and disliked, they may be on a path toward derailment or narrowing their opportunities for promotion. A leader who fails to delegate may be seen by others as a micromanager or someone who doesn't want to empower others and doesn't trust his or her team.

Case Studies: Two Wrongs and a Right

Consider the following examples of three leaders—Michael, Dominic, and Kavita—two of whom are ineffective as delegators and one who gets it right. Do you see yourself in any of the stories?

Our first case study is of Michael, a midlevel leader in a large organization. His workspace is piled high with papers, and his calendar is filled with meetings. He does not leave the office until late, and he comes in first thing in the morning. Michael always tells his boss that there is no issue with his workload and he is fine with the way things are. "No one can do what I do, and if I hand it off to other people, they will just get it wrong," Michael says. "I need to do everything myself, but there is only so much I can do. If I pass something on and someone botches it, my job will be the one on the line. I can't afford for that to happen."

Our second case study is of Dominic, a senior-level leader. He has been moved forward rapidly in his company and is now in a developmental assignment outside of his technical competence. Dominic can often be found at his desk with his head in his hands. "I just don't know what to do," Dominic says. "I understand the company, what it does, and where it wants to go. My old boss got me this job, saying it would move me forward. Now I am just lost. I have a lot of technical experts and all this work, but I just don't know how to get it across to them. In my old job, I did all this myself and it worked out great. Now there is just too much. When I tell people to do something, they just go off, do it, and stop. I want them to show commitment and innovation—otherwise, I end up doing the task all over again. So I just do it myself."

Finally there is Kavita, a seasoned leader who is ready to take the next leadership step in her organization. "I try to get at least one to two hours of thinking time in every day," Kavita says. "When I first started, I couldn't do it, but I realized that it was key to my effectiveness. If I can get one or two hours a day just to think about what is happening and where my team and I need to be next, it helps. But it isn't easy. I have to analyze each task I receive and then make sure the right person is assigned to it. We talk about the task, and my favorite question is to ask what the task will look like when it is completed. We go over how much authority they have, the role they want me to play, and when and how we will review progress. That's kind of it, really. They know I am available for questions at any time, and we set up a timeline for checking in on progress. It makes my team happier when I have this time to think because they know it benefits them in the long run."

Can you identify some roadblocks that Michael and Dominic are encountering? Are any of these obstacles familiar in your own work?

To achieve the potential benefits of delegation, leaders need to be competent at finding a good balance between autonomy and control.

The Delegation Cycle

Effective delegation is not a linear process—it is a cycle. It starts with the leader and involves four key steps. First, leaders have to understand their preferences for delegation. Second, they need to understand their people; this helps provide them with the intellectual resources to accomplish the task. Third, they need to understand the task, and more specifically, the purpose of the task. And fourth, they have to work with the individual or team to share the process for assessing and rewarding the accomplishment of the task. When the leader is at the center of the four steps, a reinforcing circle of authority and trust is created.

Figure 1. The Delegation Cycle

Preferences

Since the delegation process begins and ends with the leader, the leader needs to clearly understand his or her preferences for delegation. You can gain some insights into your preferences by looking back at the scorecard earlier in this book. How did you answer the questions? Do you constantly hold things back, or do you share information with others? Do you learn about others and their desires and strengths? Do you know your team and what it would like to achieve?

Leaders who are strongest at delegation are those who are dedicated to using the tasks that come across their desks as development opportunities for others. To do this, they have to understand and conquer their fear of assigning tasks to others. This fear may stem from the culture of the organization, past failures, or the kind of concerns discussed earlier—such as worrying that not doing a task on their own will lead to failure. Having conquered this fear, they seek opportunities for the personal development of those they lead. Good leaders offer their subordinates a chance to lead and a chance to learn while tackling difficult tasks.

Leaders who delegate effectively know themselves and what they want. Ask yourself: Are you a stickler for time, or do you let people accomplish tasks on their own timeline as long as they reach the goal? Do you want constant updates or just a report now and then? Do you consider achievement to be all about the numbers, or is strategy more important? How do you move toward your goals? Will you let the person or team assigned the task determine the process, or must you have it done your way?

The key is to know what you want and to tell the person or team to whom you are assigning the task. This important conversation greatly lessens the chances of your becoming frustrated and helps the individual or team understand your behavior and your needs.

You have to prioritize your workload and understand what is important to you and your organization before you delegate. When you do this, it tells everyone on your team what you think is important and conveys that when you do choose to delegate a critical task, the person or team responsible has been offered a true test of your trust.

You can gain additional insight into your delegating preferences by filling in the blanks of the following statements:

- The three things I do best as a leader are _____
  _____
  _____.

- The three things I can best delegate are _____
  _____
  _____.

- When I delegate a task, I prefer that the assignee _____
  _____
  _____.

- As the delegator, I want to be kept informed of _____
  _____
  _____.

- To me, success in a task is when the assignee _____
  _____
  _____.

Leaders who are strongest at delegation are those who are dedicated to using the tasks that come across their desks as development opportunities for others.

People

One reason many leaders do not delegate is that they do not like having other people do things for them. They may fear that delegation will lead to poor work quality and damaged credibility. This fear stems from misunderstanding their workforce. By truly understanding the people they manage, they can effectively identify the individuals to whom they should or should not delegate specific tasks. Effective delegating involves assigning people tasks, responsibilities, and duties that match their knowledge, skills, abilities, and interests. It involves giving them tasks, responsibilities, and duties that will help them develop and advance. The key is to frame delegation as a positive rather than a risk.

Effective delegators know that making others look good is evidence to their bosses that they can build capacity in the workforce and recognize the skills and talents of others. It also shows that if they are promoted to a new position, they will leave behind a team that will be able to handle important tasks. Leaders who think ahead and develop their team through delegated tasks are valued by any organization.

Here are some questions you can ask the individuals on your team to gain insight into their strengths, weaknesses, and desires:

- What do you do well?
- What do you do poorly?
- What kind of projects would you like to work on?
- What would you like to be doing that you are not doing now?
- In five years, where would you like to be in the organization?
- What is something not on your résumé that you think might be helpful to our team and company as we move forward?

- What support do you need in order to succeed?
- How can I personally support you or find others who can do so?

Task

Now that you have gained a thorough understanding of your team and its individual members, it's time to define the task at hand. Successful leaders take the time to carefully consider the task, asking critical process-oriented questions and, most important, pinpointing the purpose of the task. When a leader effectively matches the purpose of a task with a team's or individual's beliefs and goals, it becomes an opportunity for development.

In most organizations, tasks are not assigned unless there is a clear purpose to the task. Only then will resources be allotted to accomplish the task. It's important to understand the difference between the terms *task* and *purpose*. The task is what must be accomplished. The purpose is the reason that the task is being done—it gives meaning to the task. The two terms may look different at different levels of the organization. At higher levels, the purpose of the work may be clear ("we need to expand" or "we need to have safety in all our plants"), but the specific tasks needed to accomplish the work may be less clear. At lower levels, the task might be clear, but the purpose might be less well understood. That's why it's critical for the delegator to communicate a sharply defined task and purpose to the individual or team assigned the task.

One way to do this is to think of the task in terms of journalism's five Ws and one H—who, what, when, where, why, and how. Who is going to tackle the task? What must be done to achieve success? When should the task start and be completed? Where should the assignee go for information and assistance? Why is the task being undertaken? How will you be involved in the process?

Now add an R—resources. Doing this demonstrates your commitment to the individual or team because it clarifies your understanding of the resource situation and how they will need to make use of it. Resources include more than just money; they might include time, subject matter experts, other members of the team, your time, and your network of contacts. All of these are important resources you should consider when assigning the task.

Gaining commitment from the individual or team assigned the task comes from their understanding the meaning behind the task and their willingness to go beyond the original assignment if necessary to accomplish the purpose. Many leaders end up frustrated when a task is technically complete but hasn't quite met the mark envisioned. This is usually because the leader did not effectively communicate to the assignee the explicit purpose of the task.

Being clear on the task and purpose is just the beginning of the actual delegation. Now you need to think about what you are going to tell the individual or team when you assign the task. By doing this, you are providing the assignee with the authority needed to accomplish the task. Like all good management, providing this authority is a process. Engage the assignee in a dialogue and consider these factors:

- How is responsibility allocated? The delegator is responsible for the overall accomplishment, but who on the assignee's team is responsible for what part of the task? How will the assignee report to you, and when?

- How will the delegator hold the assignee accountable? Will it be through personal meetings, phone calls, e-mails, or reports from other departments? This is absolutely key to establishing a sound foundation for communication.

- Who needs to be consulted? This is important in establishing boundaries; it tells the assignee whom they can or should speak with or work with in accomplishing the task.

- Who needs to be informed, and how? Understanding the informal requirements of information flow will help the assignee internalize the importance of the task. As the delegator, you must be crystal clear not only about who must be informed but also about the best way you can be reached for questions, support, and information.

Assess and Reward

When you assign a task to an individual or team, how do you follow up? Do you follow up on the task itself or on how the assignee accomplished or is accomplishing the task? Good delegators do both, and they do it with the help of the person or team assigned the task. Once a distinct understanding of the task and its purpose has been established, the assignee needs to gain a clear understanding of what is important to you in order to accomplish the task.

Up to this point, you have read about providing authority to the right person or team and assigning an unambiguous task that is clearly tied to its purpose. Determining how you will assess the process used by assignees and their success at achieving tasks reflects how much you are going to trust them to accomplish those tasks. Will you require them to report to you after every step of the project, or will you just ask for a weekly rundown? Will you develop a series of benchmarks you want them to meet with regard to the project? The importance of establishing an assessment method is that it demonstrates your trust in the assignees' use of the authority you have granted them.

At CCL, we are often asked how a leader can give someone the responsibility to accomplish a task. We have found that in actuality, you can never give someone such responsibility because the ultimate responsibility for the assigned task falls to the leader. What you can do is provide the authority to accomplish the task. In the final analysis, this is really what delegation is. You have responsibilities as a leader, and you are, in essence, delegating the authority to someone else to accomplish the tasks tied to those responsibilities. How can you identify individuals who are ready to manage such authority? It starts with hiring. "Hire the people you trust, and trust them" is a wise adage. You have hired people you consider capable and trustworthy, so trust them with tough jobs. If you did not hire them, your job as a leader is to develop them, learn from them, and put them in positions that will stretch their development and help them grow.

Providing the authority to make delegation happen is one of the areas where many leaders push back the most. Why? Because they are being asked to share leadership with subordinates in ways that seemingly go against what has made them successful. Looking at delegation through a lens of maintaining responsibility while offering others authority provides a new perspective on the role of the leader.

Should leaders delegate in a crisis situation? In some cases, that is the best time to delegate. Relinquishing authority and giving employees considerable autonomy can boost innovation. In a crisis you need all the good ideas you can get, and giving others the task of helping you find those ideas demonstrates your trust in them at a critical time.

By knowing their people, effective leaders have a grasp of who can handle more authority and who can handle less. It is more art than science, but following are some thoughts on how you can help others accept greater authority and accomplish more than they thought possible.

Before the conversation with the assignee:

- Determine what level of authority you want to provide the assignee. Be prepared during the conversation to provide more or less authority.

- Understand in your mind the task and purpose of the delegation.

- Picture in your mind what success will look like. Be prepared to explain this to the assignee.

When you meet with the assignee:

- Define the task and purpose; be as clear as possible.
- Tell the assignee your perspective on what successful completion of the task will look like.
- Tell the assignee why you selected him or her for the task.
- Ask the assignee how he or she thinks the task should be done.
- Have a dialogue about the approach going forward, and provide alternative solutions and approaches.
- Schedule how you would like the assignee to check in with you.
- Help the assignee understand priorities during accomplishment of the task, and make sure you are available in accordance with the agreed-upon schedule.

If you accomplish these things before and during the meeting, the assessment part can be easy. Your goal going forward is to see where the assignee is with the project. Working with the notes from the initial dialogue, the delegator might ask for an overview of the task and its progress, then look for more detail with the following questions:

- This is where we are now—where would you like to be?
- What might be keeping you from getting there?
- What resources do you need?
- What can I do to help?
- How are you doing?
- How do you feel about this project?

The last two questions are often missing from a project review, but they provide information that is key to the successful accomplishment of the task. Understanding the mind-set of the assignee is as important as providing resources. Assignees are the people who have been given your authority to get something done. If they are upset, frustrated, angry, or confused, or if they have gone so far as to give up, their attitude is going to reflect negatively on your leadership and credibility. If they don't understand the task, are apathetic about the purpose of the task, have lost faith in the process, or find themselves overwhelmed with the burden of the task, their lack of support will reflect on your leadership. You must take the time to follow up on any issues that may be affecting the assignee's ability to accomplish what you have assigned.

Once the task has been successfully accomplished, it's time to think about how to reward the assignee. Celebrations can accomplish many different ends. They offer closure, recognition, and feedback. Key to deciding on rewards is understanding the people who have accomplished the tasks and what might mean the most to them. Some people like to receive a certificate or diploma in front of their coworkers. For many employees, the best reward is when a boss they respect spends time with them. During this time they might go over the task and talk about the process used to achieve the purpose. Other rewards can include small mementos or a personal lunch with you.

Everyone likes to be recognized for working hard. This is why the reward phase is such a critical step in the delegation process. It signifies that the task is over, the purpose has been met, and the assignee has been recognized.

When Things Go Wrong

Sometimes, despite all your preparation and discussions during the delegation process, things go wrong. How will you handle this? Will you scream at the assignee? Will you avoid confrontation? Will you seek to place blame on the assignee? Or will you try to find out what happened, why it happened, and what needs to be done to fix it? Good leaders engage their employees in these conversations—not to impose blame but to reinforce trust and find better ideas. Using a calm voice and manner, help the assignee see what happened and point out ways to fix the problem.

Good coaching skills are essential for effective delegation. The worst delegators are those who simply say, "It's off my desk." The best are those who develop a relationship with the assignees through a dialogue about the task, describe the purpose with clarity, challenge the assignees with something new, give them the resources and authority they need, and support them during the journey through appropriate attention, conversation, and autonomy.

Last Words

Empowering is allowing a person to have substantial responsibility and discretion for meaningful and important tasks, providing the information and resources needed to make and implement decisions, and trusting the person to solve problems and make decisions without getting prior approval. An important aspect of empowering is delegation, which involves assigning new projects and responsibilities to individuals or a team and providing the authority, resources, direction, and support needed to achieve the expected results.

Employees are likely to have more commitment to implementing a decision when they feel they have ownership of the decision and are accountable for its consequences. People often speak fondly of leaders who gave them empowering opportunities to push the envelope of their abilities to accomplish difficult tasks and become better people as a result.

Employees are likely to have more commitment to implementing a decision when they feel they have ownership of the decision and are accountable for its consequences.

A senior leader who was participating in one of CCL's leadership development programs recently delivered a succinct message that defines the key to effective delegation and avoiding micromanagement. She told the class of senior executives, leaders who had decades of experience and who ran some of the most powerful organizations in the country, "As a leader, do the work only you can do...[and] empower someone else to do the rest."

As you proceed to empower others by giving them opportunities to excel, make sure you understand why you are handing these tasks off. The task may be a strategic priority you want to have more information about. It may be something that needs to be done but you don't have the time or the requisite knowledge or skills to do it. It may be a developmental opportunity for an emerging leader. Know why you should not be handling the task and why you are offering others the chance to work on it.

When you are adept at knowing your people, clearly communicating to them the task and its purpose, giving them the resources and support to achieve the task, helping them with the process, and rewarding their success, then the assignees come back to you wanting more, and you know you have become an effective delegator. It takes practice and patience. You may not know it, but others are waiting for the challenge. Your task is to provide it to them.

Background

The Center for Creative Leadership's understanding of effective delegation and leadership strategies is drawn from many different sources. These include CCL's own research on how successful leaders learn from experience and from evaluation of their leadership experience, proven research works in the field, experiences in the classroom and learning from participants, and the experiences of leaders outside the classroom. The author of this guidebook also drew on more than 25 years of experience in working with leaders to provide case studies and insights reflecting a number of delegation experiences.

CCL research has found that the most common reasons for leader derailment—that is, being fired or demoted, or reaching a career plateau—are specific performance problems, including failure to delegate or build a team. It has also identified four requisite skills for leaders of the future: leading employees, managing change, building and mending relationships, and employing participative leadership.

Of the four, leading employees is the most important skill. Leaders who are effective in this area excel in the following three ways:

- They delegate and develop. They are willing to delegate important tasks and decisions. This is done as an effective management technique but, more important, as a means to develop employees. Providing challenge and opportunity builds skill, experience, and confidence. As a result, effective leaders surround themselves with talented people.

- They provide feedback. They are honest and consistent in communicating expectations and results. The feedback—both positive and negative—is provided promptly.

- They motivate. They reward hard work and dedication to excellence. They willingly explain, answer questions, and patiently listen to concerns.

In addition, a team working on CCL's initiative in technology-driven learning recently had a conversation with the aim of creating an online module on learning to delegate. A key learning of this panel is that many resources are more about shared leadership than about delegation per se. Although shared leadership is a form of delegation, it may be less appropriate for entry-level leaders than for more advanced leaders.

Delegation is a difficult topic in leadership because it involves providing others the guidance to perform critical tasks and giving them the authority to do so. In current literature, the difference between authority to perform a task and responsibility for its accomplishment are often not identified or discussed. Although this difference is covered at length in many different manuals related to the military, the civilian leadership community has not yet fully made the distinction. This guidebook is intended to introduce readers to the distinction that giving someone the authority to accomplish a task does not mean relinquishing the responsibility for its accomplishment.

Suggested Resources

Amar, A. D., Hentrich, C., & Hlupic, V. (2009). To be a better leader, give up authority. *Harvard Business Review, 87*(12), 22–24.

Barrett, A. (2008, June 19). Matching the right people to the right jobs. *BusinessWeek*. Retrieved from www.businessweek.com

Drath, W. (2003). Leading together: Complex challenges require a new approach. *Leadership in Action, 23*(1), 3–7.

Genett, D. M. (2004). If you want it done right, you don't have to do it yourself! The power of effective delegation. Fresno, CA: Quill Driver Books.

Heller, R. (1997). *How to delegate* (Essential Managers Series). New York, NY: DK.

Krohe, J., Jr. (2010). If you love your people, set them free. *Conference Board Review, 47*(5), 28–37.

Schneider, B. (2004, October 22). Learning to delegate. *Entrepreneur*. Retrieved from www.entrepreneur.com

Ordering Information

TO GET MORE INFORMATION, TO ORDER OTHER IDEAS INTO ACTION GUIDEBOOKS, OR TO FIND OUT ABOUT BULK-ORDER DISCOUNTS, PLEASE CONTACT US BY PHONE AT 336-545-2810 OR VISIT OUR ONLINE BOOKSTORE AT WWW.CCL.ORG/GUIDEBOOKS.

CPSIA information can be obtained
at www.ICGtesting.com
Printed in the USA
LVHW020809010721
691501LV00004B/15